THE LANGUAGE OF DIVINITY

A bouquet of spiritual poems

Compiled and edited by

Abhishek Thakkar

&

Purba Chakraborty

Published by

Notion Press

Compiler + Editor:

Abhishek Thakkar & Purba Chakraborty

Poetry (English)

In this book:

Dedicated to 6

Hari-Hara 8

Dr. Amrita Pani 8

A Tale of Ancient Love 12

Gunjan Chauhan 12

My Divinity 15

Himanshu Parida 15

Awake 19

Abhishek Thakkar 19

Appo Deepo Bhavah 22

Abhishek Thakkar 22

O Krishna! 26

Abhishek Thakkar 26

The Greatest Wealth 30

Abhishek Thakkar 30

Kali will Rise 33

Abhishek Thakkar 33

Krishna 38

Purba Chakraborty 38

My Eternal Mother 42

Purba Chakraborty 42

Sapphire Sky..45

Purba Chakraborty..45

Taming the Tempest..48

Purba Chakraborty..48

Greatest Musician..50

Purba Chakraborty..50

The Coronet..53

Andrew Marvell..53

On a Drop of Dew..55

Andrew Marvell..55

On his blindness..59

John Milton..59

I know that He Exists..62

Emily Dickinson..62

I shall know why – when Time is over..63

Emily Dickinson..63

The Soul's distinct connection..65

Emily Dickinson..65

The Bible is an Antique Volume..66

Emily Dickinson..66

The Tyger..69

William Blake..69

The Education of Nature..72

William Wordsworth..72

Holy Sonnet 14..76

John Donne..76

Where the Mind is without Fear..............................79

Rabindranath Tagore..79

Stream of Life..81

Rabindranath Tagore..81

When the Heart is hard and parched up..................83

Rabindranath Tagore..83

About 'The Language of Divinity'............................86

Dedicated to

The lotus feet of Lord Krishna and Radha Rani

And

Guru Vyas Saheb (devotee of Ma Amba)

Hari-Hara

Dr. Amrita Pani

In Krishna's heart, Shiva resides,
A cosmic dance, where love abides.
With matted locks, a silent grace,
Hara finds his home in Hari's embrace.
And in Shiva's heart, Krishna dwells,
A flute's sweet song, a love that swells.
One blue of night, a heavenly hue,
The other sky's expanse, forever true.
From Shiva's Tandava to Krishna's gentle flute,
their divine melodies heal and transmute.
They dance in unity, a timeless rhyme,
Bound by the thread of love, through space and time.

One fierce, one gentle, both divine,
One in Samsara, one in trance.
A peacock feather, Trident's might,
Of love and wisdom, shining light.
The flute's soft song, a yearning call,
Echoes the Damru's rhythmic thrall.
Hari and Hara, my heart's desire,
Two divinities, my soul's fire.
Celestial duo, divine and grand,
Forever intertwined, they eternally stand.
In Shiva's stillness, Krishna's grace,
A love divine, I find my place.
One in devotion, one in liberation,
Hari-Hara whispers, 'Find your peace.'

About Dr. Amrita Pani

While Dr. Amrita Pani's day job is that of a business administration professor, her true calling is as a writer, storyteller, poet, and novelist. She has a prolific publishing history, with works in both fiction and travel memoir. She made her literary debut in 2021 with the release of her romance novel, An Evening in Izmir with a Cup of Tea.

A Tale of Ancient Love

Gunjan Chauhan

In the ancient streets of Vrindavan,
Where time's whispers echo,
where souls began,
A unique feeling, a bond unseen,
As if a long-lost love, now found serene.

Four years ago,
amidst the crowd,
In your presence,
my heart aloud,
Sought to catch a glimpse, to be near,
A joy unknown, a love sincere.

Our connection,
not bound by years,
But by the echoes of ancient tears,
A meeting ordained, in paths unknown,
A love that in hearts has always grown.

Tears, like rivers,
flowed that day,
As if destiny had its say,

In the journey of souls, intertwined,
An ancient love, forever defined.

Walking out that door, a world anew,
In Vrindavan's embrace, our love true,
Transformed into verse, this tale of ours,
In the heart's whispers, amidst ancient towers.

About Gunjan Chauhan

Gunjan Chauhan was born on October 2, 2002, in Auraiya, Uttar Pradesh. She is currently pursuing a master's degree at Banaras Hindu University. With a keen interest in writing, Gunjan enjoys reading, crafting short stories, and composing poetry.

My Divinity

Himanshu Parida

All my life I have tried to be devotional
I have tried to see everything divine;
For me Sky is the artefact of God
And Air at God's will flowing.

I find rivers to run to a divine destination
That is Sea
I see in my divinity a larger space
Which cannot be filled by the air or sea.

I see flowers turning to fruit
And get filled with elixir of life
At God's will
I see in every human being,
A hope of life blessed by divine.

Sometimes, when I close my eyes

A different world appears before me
There are also flowers and foliage
But they live there permanently without
decay.

Being stupefied in wonder, I pray
I pray to someone who I do not know
But praise everything He does for me.

Something I imagine in my mind
What my vision cannot capture,
I hear some music which my ears
Are not able to decipher
but still, I enjoy and enjoy
many things imaginable.

About Himanshu Parida

Himanshu Parida is a known name in Odia contemporary writings of Criticism, poems and stories. He is a post graduate in English Literature from Utkal University, Bhubaneswar. He has already published six books of poems, three collection of stories and three books on Literary Criticism. His book in English 'Trivial Thoughts' has been recently published. After retirement from State Bank of India, he has devoted his full time in literary activities.

Awake

Abhishek Thakkar

Awaken from this slumber.
Arise and sleep no more.
We sleep with our eyes open.
We don't see the Real within the Unreal world.

Unreal is often misinterpreted as a delusion.
In the spiritual world, it means a temporary reality.
One moment, I am sad and, in another moment, I feel ecstatic.
How can sadness or ecstasy be Real?
This is what I mean by the word 'unreal'.

They are temporary truths.
They are fleeting emotions.

"Awaken and seek God within you."
Says my Gurudev Paramhansa Yogananda.
It is not a treasure which can only be inherited by a few.

"Pray constantly to the Heavenly Father.
You are His own child and not a beggar."

Pray because you have so much to be thankful for.
Pray because it brings you closer to Him.

Meditate on His mantras, holy names and His divine stories.
Meditate on Him who rules the lands and the seas.

Our Lord is not a vengeful Lord.
Our God loves us despite our shortcomings.

When we pray, He listens.
But we should pray not merely for bread but for the bread of Life.

Jesus is the bread of Life.
Whoever follows His instructions finds new Life.

Awaken from the sleep of ignorance.
Read Bible, Gita, Quran and destroy your arrogance.

Ego is the wall between us and God.

Why is the wall given more importance than
the Lord?

It's high time that we give up laziness.
It's high time that we relinquish our
craziness.

Awaken from this slumber now.
Enlightenment cannot wait.
Enlightenment cannot wait.

Appo Deepo Bhavah

Abhishek Thakkar

Don't depend on anyone for alleviating your suffering
Rely on yourself no matter what each situation brings

Making oneself self-reliant is what Buddhism teaches
A life based on scientific and critical thinking is what Buddha preaches

Buddha's sermons are a tool
Buddha isn't just a person but a state of realization that can even be attained by a fool

Buddhahood is perhaps harder to attain for men and women who are too obstinate
Fools are blessed with no attachment to beliefs is what Buddha would like to state

He rejected the Vedas
He rejected the caste system

He saw through the politics of priests
He couldn't tolerate religious corruption

He loved each living entity as His own body
For Him, no one was His brother but every
person was part of His own body

He was silent on the question of God
Some say that He even rejected the idea of a
Heavenly Lord

Maybe this is what makes Buddha unique
even in Hinduism
He is considered the incarnation of Vishnu
who gave equivalent space to agnosticism
and atheism

To stop animal sacrifices was his prime
motive
To stop violence against each living entity,
his own life he could give

He was supremely compassionate
He was completely pure and also passionate

He was committed to intellectual honesty
He also believed in the path of experience
and subjectivity

He taught us to be bold and fearless
He taught us to give up desire and worry less
Looking at His picture still gives inexplicable peace to everyone
There is something so compelling about him that creates awe and admiration in everyone

We have to learn so much from His life and death
He taught us the power of courage and importance of our breath.

I wish more of us could be like Him and be our true selves
Attaining Nirvana is more important than borrowed answers in the bookshelves.

O Krishna!

Abhishek Thakkar

O Krishna!
I think of the indwelling beauty
of your name.
When I meditate on it,
I just want more devotion to you
and no more fame.

O Govinda!
Bless me with
more devotion to You.
You are our best friend
and yours is the love which is true.

O Krishna!
You dwell in everyone's heart.
O Madhusudana!
The world is formed by your energies and
we are its parts.

Many amongst us are lost
in this endless labyrinth of materialism.
May we remember You and

see the world through the Krishna
Consciousness prism.

For us, the world is
composed of dualities and binaries.
But you help us see the world of
transcendence
beyond the sufferings and the glees.

Friend or foe,
both of them are equal in your eyes.
But you protect your devotees personally
whenever he or she cries.

We yearn for your love
and fail to understand its depth
Your sky-like love
has endless breadth.

You call out to us
through the scripture
You remind us of your
immanent presence in nature.

It's we who get
entangled in the knots of illusion
It's we who give up seeking You
just after some confusions.

We have been so lazy
We have been so crazy

We think of ourselves as the enjoyers
We think of ourselves as the doers

The truth is we are the instruments
you play through your lotus-like lips.
Forgetting you, we complain about
being under illusion's grips.

May we remember You continuously
who is the true source of bliss, knowledge
and eternal existence
Happiness in material life is a mirage and
happiness in spiritual life has the luminosity
of a thousand suns.

The Greatest Wealth

Abhishek Thakkar

My mental peace is my Shakti Peeth
My positive attitude is my Kaal Bhairav

I am fiercely committed
towards guarding my mental peace.

From the strands of Lord Shiva,
Kaal Bhairav is born to protect the
sacrosanct parts of Divine Mother.
From the strands of me,
positive decisions are born to take care of
my holy harmonious Being.

Taking care of oneself isn't just one's right
but a duty.
Taking care of oneself is a verb possessing
tremendous beauty.

I am a spark of that effulgent Infinity.
I am the home of indwelling strength and
serenity.

I welcome those who love me selflessly
I applaud those who detest me honestly.

But I have no room for hypocrites who
stab me in the back
Compassion for fake friends is something I
happily lack.

My mental peace is my Shakti peeth.
My positive attitude is my Kaal Bhairav.

I have no space for those who are constantly
sending me negative vibrations.
I have no space for those who rejoice in my
tribulations.

I avoid a conflict and keep a distance as
much as I can.
But if the situation demands me to fight, I
don't yield to unmanliness.

There is no space for weakness and
negativity in the world of Shiva and Parvati.
I don't allow any harmful behaviour in my
heart's sacred territory.

Kali will Rise

Abhishek Thakkar

When *bhoomi* cried and
complained about man's greed,
Vishnu was enraged and decided to slay the
miscreants who committed atrocious deeds.

Earth in all its ways was munificent and
compassionate.
But man became egotistical and overly
passionate.

Mother Earth kept on giving selflessly.
And, man possessed by his covetousness
kept on taking selfishly.

There seemed to be no end.
Mother Earth was distraught and she had no
friend.

So, she took the form of a cow
and turned to the cowherd Vishnu.
God promised to take various avatars
and put an end to the cruelty that had grew.

Man didn't realize the extent of damage he
had done to his mother.
His pursuit of sense-gratification never
seemed to wither.

Man followed the law of the jungles
and dominated the earth through
exploitation.
Driven by avarice,
he set out on a series of voyages to conquer
all the nations.

Humility became a weakness.
People gave up gentleness and meekness.

The one who oppressed others was
venerated.
Injustice and the rate of crimes accelerated.

This story is a story of our blue planet.
But I would like to remind you all that each
one amongst us is also a planet.

My heart is my sacred *bhoomi* and holy
territory.
Cried it has many times when it met deceit
and hypocrisy.

I have let friends trample on my heart
because I was so devoted and loving.
I have let so many people disappoint me
because I was generous and forgiving.

Many of my own loved ones tried to harm
me mentally.
Some of them even tried to manipulate me
psychologically.

And, that's when my heart or Gauri
refused to endure the asura or demoniac
behaviour.
Gauri didn't ask for Vishnu's help this time
and set out as Kali to fight for her.

My heart didn't succumb to the mental
violence
committed by others anymore.
I tuned myself with the omnipresence of
God
and felt the infinite strength I had in my
core.

Gauri or my heart is no more fragile as is
often perceived.
She is Kali from whom boldness and
fearlessness are conceived.

About Abhishek Thakkar

Abhishek Thakkar is an author, teacher and an entrepreneur. He has authored 5 books till now and he is also a contributing author to more than 15 anthologies of poetry and short stories.

He has also contributed research articles, poems and book reviews in international journals and reputed magazines such as International Journal of English Language and Literature, The Literary Herald Journal and the LLP Magazine.

His latest book 'Age of Chaucer (BOOK 1)' is an academic e-book which is written specially for the students of English Literature. He is the co-compiler and co-editor of ‘The Language of Love’ and ‘The Language of Divinity’ poetry books.

Krishna

Purba Chakraborty

In the words of Bhagavad Geeta

In the melody of flute

In the reverberation of Om,

I hear you, Krishna.

In the blue-green hues of a peacock feather

In the dark monsoon clouds

In the amber glow of every sunrise and sunset

I see you, Krishna.

In the kirtan of devotees

In the colors of Holi

In every beat of my heart

I feel you, Krishna.

With your name,

Begins the fountain of happiness

With your thought

Erupts the ocean of peace

You are both the journey and the destination

Without the nectar of Your Holy name,
Krishna

Life is but a long exile

Bereft of purpose and meaning

Bless me, Krishna

That when the time comes for

My soul to leave the body,

The last word I utter is Your Holy name.

My Eternal Mother

Purba Chakraborty

I lost my mother
When I was a child;
From a tender rose in a garden,
I became a flower wild-
Abandoned
Neglected
Independent.

My mother was my
Nourisher, Healer, Protector
Blanket of Peace
Ocean of Love
Sky of Freedom;
Losing her to death
Left me with a life full of questions
I became a seeker
In search of answers.

I waged war with Destiny
Looked for her love everywhere

Craved for rain in the desert
Battled with Fate;
I was getting chained in the labyrinth of pain
Until one evening on Durga Ashtami
Amid the symphony of conch shells
Reciting of chants
Fragrance of incense,
I heard a melodious voice
Speaking from within me-
“My Dear Child!
Don’t you realize it is me,
Who is healing, nourishing, and protecting
you
Birth after birth, day after day
In the forms of many Earthly mothers and
Nature?”

With a jolt, I awakened from a long slumber
I gazed into the eyes of the huge idol
of Maa Durga;

My eyes glistened with tears
As I discovered an ocean of Love
Overflowing in my heart.
“Yes! There dwells my Eternal Mother
Like a fool, I was looking outside
For droplets of love.”

I embraced the Divine Mother in my heart
Knowing I can never be separated from her.

Sapphire Sky

Purba Chakraborty

The resplendent sapphire sky

Streaked with

White fluffy cumulus clouds

At one corner

And grey dense nimbus clouds

At another corner

Hints a message from the beyond

for my weary grief-stricken heart

~ You are the ever-vast sky,

made in the image of God

You encompass both

Sadness and Happiness

that add beauty to your canvas;

Let the agonising thoughts

pour as rain from your eyes;

Now float with ecstasy

like the white cumulus clouds.

Taming the Tempest

Purba Chakraborty

The tempest tells me

Break! Break! Break!

I am here to crumble you into pieces

Why don't you fear me?

I am colossal and overpowering

Break! Break! Break!

I look into the eye of the tempest

And say

Try! Try! Try!

Yet you'll fail and fail

My God is bigger than you

Way more colossal

And way more powerful

My God is there in every atom of

the storm

Try as much as you can

You cannot drown me

As my God is sailing my ship.

Greatest Musician

Purba Chakraborty

I was stringing my instrument
To play the right chord
When the gushing waterfall,
The rustle of leaves,
And the chirping of birds
Blended to form a magical harmony.
I humbly bowed down before The greatest
musician- Nature.

About Purba Chakraborty

Purba Chakraborty is an author of 7 books. She has written 3 novels (Canvas of a Mind, The Hidden Letters, Walking in the streets of Love and Destiny), 1 novella (You Came like Autumn) and 3 poetry books (Mythological Monologues, Letters from the Soul, The Heart Listens to No One).

She is the founder and CEO of Learning Literature with Purba. She is the editor-in-chief of The LLP Magazine. She is an educator, YouTuber, Podcaster, blogger, and a content writer. She is the co-compiler and co-editor of 'The Language of Love' and 'The Language of Divinity' poetry collections.

The Coronet

Andrew Marvell

When for the thorns with which I long, too long,
With many a piercing wound,
My Saviour's head have crowned,
I seek with garlands to redress that wrong:
Through every garden, every mead,
I gather flowers (my fruits are only flowers),
Dismantling all the fragrant towers
That once adorned my shepherdess's head.
And now when I have summed up all my store,
Thinking (so I myself deceive)
So rich a chaplet thence to weave
As never yet the King of Glory wore:
Alas, I find the serpent old
That, twining in his speckled breast,
About the flowers disguised does fold,
With wreaths of fame and interest.
Ah, foolish man, that wouldst debase with them,
And mortal glory, Heaven's diadem!
But Thou who only couldst the serpent tame,

Either his slippery knots at once untie;
And disentangle all his winding snare;
Or shatter too with him my curious frame,
And let these wither, so that he may die,
Though set with skill and chosen out with care:
That they, while Thou on both their spoils dost tread,
May crown thy feet, that could not crown thy head.

On a Drop of Dew

Andrew Marvell

See how the orient dew,
Shed from the bosom of the morn
Into the blowing roses,
Yet careless of its mansion new,
For the clear region where 'twas born
Round in itself incloses:
And in its little globe's extent,
Frames as it can its native element.
How it the purple flow'r does slight,
Scarce touching where it lies,
But gazing back upon the skies,
Shines with a mournful light,
Like its own tear,
Because so long divided from the sphere.
Restless it rolls and unsecure,
Trembling lest it grow impure,
Till the warm sun pity its pain,
And to the skies exhale it back again.
So the soul, that drop, that ray
Of the clear fountain of eternal day,
Could it within the human flow'r be seen,
Remembering still its former height,

Shuns the sweet leaves and blossoms green,
And recollecting its own light,
Does, in its pure and circling thoughts, express
The greater heaven in an heaven less.
In how coy a figure wound,
Every way it turns away:
So the world excluding round,
Yet receiving in the day,
Dark beneath, but bright above,
Here disdaining, there in love.
How loose and easy hence to go,
How girt and ready to ascend,
Moving but on a point below,
It all about does upwards bend.
Such did the manna's sacred dew distill,
White and entire, though congealed and chill,
Congealed on earth : but does, dissolving, run
Into the glories of th' almighty sun.

About Andrew Marvell

Andrew Marvell was an English metaphysical poet, satirist and politician who sat in the House of Commons at various times between 1659 and 1678. During the Commonwealth period he was a colleague and friend of John Milton.

On his blindness

John Milton

When I consider how my light is spent,
Ere half my days, in this dark world and wide,
And that one Talent which is death to hide
Lodged with me useless, though my Soul more bent
To serve therewith my Maker, and present
My true account, lest he returning chide;
"Doth God exact day-labour, light denied?"
I fondly ask. But patience, to prevent
That murmur, soon replies, "God doth not need
Either man's work or his own gifts; who best
Bear his mild yoke, they serve him best. His state
Is Kingly. Thousands at his bidding speed
And post o'er Land and Ocean without rest:
They also serve who only stand and wait."

About John Milton

John Milton was a 17th century historian, journalist and poet born on December 9th, 1608 in London, England. He was best known for his writing of *Paradise Lost.*

I know that He Exists

Emily Dickinson

I know that He exists.
Somewhere – in silence –
He has hid his rare life
From our gross eyes.

'Tis an instant's play –
'Tis a fond Ambush –
Just to make Bliss
Earn her own surprise!

But – should the play
Prove piercing earnest –
Should the glee – glaze –
In Death's – stiff – stare –

Would not the fun
Look too expensive!
Would not the jest –
Have crawled too far!

I shall know why – when Time is over

Emily Dickinson

I shall know why—when Time is over—
And I have ceased to wonder why—
Christ will explain each separate anguish
In the fair schoolroom of the sky—

He will tell me what "Peter" promised—
And I—for wonder at his woe—
I shall forget the drop of Anguish
That scalds me now—that scalds me now!

The Soul's distinct connection

Emily Dickinson

The Soul's distinct connection
With immortality
Is best disclosed by Danger
Or quick Calamity—

As Lightning on a Landscape
Exhibits Sheets of Place—
Not yet suspected—but for Flash—
And Click—and Suddenness.

The Bible is an Antique Volume

Emily Dickinson

The Bible is an antique Volume—
Written by faded men
At the suggestion of Holy Spectres—
Subjects—Bethlehem—
Eden—the ancient Homestead—
Satan—the Brigadier—
Judas—the Great Defaulter—
David—the Troubadour—
Sin—a distinguished Precipice
Others must resist—
Boys that "believe" are very lonesome—
Other Boys are "lost"—
Had but the Tale a warbling Teller—
All the Boys would come—
Orpheus' Sermon captivated—
It did not condemn—

About Emily Dickinson

Emily Dickinson was an American poet best known for her eccentric personality and her frequent themes of death and mortality. Although she was a prolific writer, only a few of her poems were published during her lifetime. Despite being mostly unknown while she was alive, her poetry—nearly 1,800 poems altogether—has become a staple of the American literary canon.

The Tyger

William Blake

Tyger Tyger, burning bright,
In the forests of the night;
What immortal hand or eye,
Could frame thy fearful symmetry?

In what distant deeps or skies.
Burnt the fire of thine eyes?
On what wings dare he aspire?
What the hand, dare seize the fire?

And what shoulder, & what art,
Could twist the sinews of thy heart?
And when thy heart began to beat.
What dread hand? & what dread feet?

What the hammer? what the chain,
In what furnace was thy brain?
What the anvil? what dread grasp.
Dare its deadly terrors clasp?

When the stars threw down their spears
And water'd heaven with their tears:
Did he smile his work to see?
Did he who made the Lamb make thee?

Tyger Tyger burning bright,
In the forests of the night:
What immortal hand or eye,
Dare frame thy fearful symmetry?

About William Blake

William Blake was an English poet, painter, and printmaker. Largely unrecognised during his life, Blake has become a seminal figure in the history of the poetry and visual art of the Romantic Age.

The Education of Nature

William Wordsworth

Three years she grew in sun and shower,
Then Nature said, "A lovelier flower
On earth was never sown;
This Child I to myself will take;
She shall be mine, and I will make
A Lady of my own.

"Myself will to my darling be
Both law and impulse: and with me
The Girl, in rock and plain,
In earth and heaven, in glade and bower,
Shall feel an overseeing power
To kindle or restrain.

"She shall be sportive as the fawn
That wild with glee across the lawn
Or up the mountain springs;
And hers shall be the breathing balm,
And hers the silence and the calm
Of mute insensate things.

"The floating clouds their state shall lend

To her; for her the willow bend;
Nor shall she fail to see
Even in the motions of the Storm
Grace that shall mould the Maiden's form
By silent sympathy.

"The stars of midnight shall be dear
To her; and she shall lean her ear
In many a secret place
Where rivulets dance their wayward round,
And beauty born of murmuring sound
Shall pass into her face.

"And vital feelings of delight
Shall rear her form to stately height,
Her virgin bosom swell;
Such thoughts to Lucy I will give
While she and I together live
Here in this happy dell."

Thus Nature spake—The work was done—
How soon my Lucy's race was run!
She died, and left to me
This heath, this calm and quiet scene;
The memory of what has been,
And never more will be.

About William Wordsworth

William Wordsworth was an English Romantic poet who, with Samuel Taylor Coleridge, helped to launch the Romantic Age in English literature with their joint publication Lyrical Ballads.

Holy Sonnet 14

John Donne

Batter my heart, three-person'd God, for you
As yet but knock, breathe, shine, and seek to mend;
That I may rise and stand, o'erthrow me, and bend
Your force to break, blow, burn, and make me new.
I, like an usurp'd town to another due,
Labor to admit you, but oh, to no end;
Reason, your viceroy in me, me should defend,
But is captiv'd, and proves weak or untrue.
Yet dearly I love you, and would be lov'd fain,
But am betroth'd unto your enemy;
Divorce me, untie or break that knot again,
Take me to you, imprison me, for I,
Except you enthrall me, never shall be free,
Nor ever chaste, except you ravish me.

About John Donne

John Donne was an English poet, scholar, soldier and secretary born into a recusant family, who later became a cleric in the Church of England. Under Royal Patronage, he was made Dean of St Paul's Cathedral in London. He is considered the preeminent representative of the metaphysical poets.

Where the Mind is without Fear

Rabindranath Tagore

Where the mind is without fear and the head
is held high
Where knowledge is free
Where the world has not been broken up
into fragments
By narrow domestic walls
Where words come out from the depth of
truth
Where tireless striving stretches its arms
towards perfection
Where the clear stream of reason has not lost
its way
Into the dreary desert sand of dead habit
Where the mind is led forward by thee
Into ever-widening thought and action
Into that heaven of freedom, my Father, let
my country awake!

Stream of Life

Rabindranath Tagore

The same stream of life that runs through
my veins night and day
runs through the world and dances in
rhythmic measures.

It is the same life that shoots in joy through
the dust of the earth
in numberless blades of grass
and breaks into tumultuous waves of leaves
and flowers.

It is the same life that is rocked in the ocean-
cradle of birth
and of death, in ebb and in flow.

I feel my limbs are made glorious by the
touch of this world of life.
And my pride is from the life-throb of ages
dancing in my blood this moment.

When the Heart is hard and parched up

Rabindranath Tagore

When the heart is hard and parched up,
come upon me with a shower of mercy.
When grace is lost from life, come with a burst of song.
When tumultuous work raises its din on all sides shutting me out from beyond, come to me, my lord of silence, with thy peace and rest.
When my beggarly heart sits crouched, shut up in a corner, break open the door, my king, and come with the ceremony of a king.
When desire blinds the mind with delusion and dust, O thou holy one, thou wakeful, come with thy light and thy thunder.

About Rabindranath Tagore

Rabindranath Tagore was a Bengali poet, writer, playwright, composer, philosopher, social reformer, and painter of the Bengal Renaissance. He reshaped Bengali literature and music as well as Indian art with Contextual Modernism in the late 19th and early 20th centuries. He was the first non-European to win the Nobel Prize in Literature in 1913 for his poetry collection 'Gitanjali'.

About 'The Language of Divinity'

'But when I found that I knew not only that there was God but that I was a child of God, when I understood that, when I comprehended that, more than that, when I internalized that, ingested that, I became courageous." ~ Maya Angelou

'The Language of Divinity' is the second poetry project by authors Abhishek Thakkar and Purba Chakraborty who are also the compilers and editors of the book. Their first poetry project 'The Language of Love' was a roaring success and gained a lot of accolades from the literary fraternity. Abhishek and Purba, hailing from two states of India, Gujarat and West Bengal respectively have been in a long-distance relationship for six years before tying the knot in 2023. After the success of 'The Language of Love', they decided to bring a book on spirituality by collaborating with some talented Indian poets and featuring some memorable poems on spirituality by classical Indian, European and American poets.

They also plan to launch many more poetry projects in the near future so that they can provide a platform to many talented poets and writers whose voice need to be heard.

If you enjoyed reading this book, kindly leave a review on Amazon and Instagram.

You can also send your feedback or review at thelanguageoflovepoetrybook@gmail.com

You can get in touch with them on Instagram at @abhishekvthakkar1010 and @purba_chakraborty

Grab a copy of The Language of Love on Amazon.

www.ingramcontent.com/pod-product-compliance
Lightning Source LLC
LaVergne TN
LVHW041131150826
845673LV00007B/2275

* 9 7 9 8 8 9 5 8 8 7 0 6 6 *